THE ROAD TO HOLINESS

Man's Way or God's Way?

E. W. BULLINGER

ISBN: 978-1-78364-502-2

www.obt.org.uk

****

The Open Bible Trust
Fordland Mount, Upper Basildon,
Reading, RG8 8LU, UK.

THE ROAD TO HOLINESS
Man's Way or God's Way?

CONTENTS

Page

The Road to Holiness 4

PREFACE

These studies by E. W. Bullinger were first written in the last years of the 19th Century. Thus what he refers to a 'The Modern Movement' relates to what had arisen in the United Kingdom at that time. However, some of the errors of that 'Modern Movement' persist today and so much of what he wrote then is relevant and helpful to the 21st Century Christian.

He refers to many journals and magazines such as *The Keswick Week, The Christian, The Life of Faith*, and the magazine he edited, *Things to Come*. None of these are still in publication.

The Road to Holiness 6

HOLINESS:

GOD'S WAY BETTER THAN MAN'S

Holiness of life and walk is God's will for His children; as it is, or should be, their own earnest desire.

God's will on this matter has been declared and revealed. "This is the will of God, even your sanctification" (1 Thess. 4:3).

God has not left His will, or the means for its accomplishment, to chance, or to be discovered at the end of this nineteenth century.

The Road to Holiness 8

GOD'S WAY

One of God's methods for securing holiness of life is by "HOPE." This hope is set upon a person – Christ (1 John 3:3). It is part of the foundation of true Christian standing to be waiting for God's Son from heaven (1 Thess. 1:9, 10). Thus, looking *for* Christ, we are, of necessity, looking *to* Christ, and are occupied *with* Christ, and in this manner, we are "conformed to His image."

> "We beholding-as-in-a mirror the glory of the Lord, ARE changed into the same image from glory to glory, even as by the Lord the Spirit". (2 Cor. 3:18)

Here is no restless effort, no anxious toiling, no spiritual dissipation, no occupation with "the ordinances of men," but occupation of heart with a heavenly object, producing a heavenly character and walk – and this by secret transmutation – without an effort! This is God's one, simple and withal efficacious method for securing the accomplishment of His will in those who believe

God as described in Rom. 5:12-8:39 and are thus counted righteous by Him.

MAN'S WAY

Now, man has always thought that he can improve on God's plans; and he has ever sought to do so, or to substitute his own for them.

As in the matter of *justification*, in Genesis 4, so in the matter of *sanctification*, "the way of Cain" is contrary to "the way of God."

This has been so from the first, and it is seen in *all* the various forms of false religion. They all say, "something in my hand I bring," though they quarrel bitterly as to what that "something" is to be. But that it is to be "*something*," they all agree about; they are all at one. True religion, on the other hand says, "*Nothing* in my hand I bring."

As it is with justification, so it is with sanctification. And those who hold that they are "justified by His grace," too often act as though they were deceived by the specious delusion that they are to be sanctified by works. Whereas Christ, of God, is made unto us sanctification, as well as righteousness (1 Cor. 1:30), and in precisely the same way. God having made His people righteous in Christ, has not afterwards left them to seek their sanctification in themselves.

MAN'S METHOD

But this is man's method. The present Holiness movement was not heard of in this country until Mr. and Mrs. Pearsall Smith brought it from America, about the year 1872. Those who know the beginning of the movement remember how the whole Evangelical body in England were "bewitched," and ran madly into the new movement, until, at the Brighton Convention, it almost collapsed, from the severe blow received in the fact of its leader giving a sad proof of the failure of his new method to secure holiness of life.

Mr. and Mrs. Pearsall Smith, after having had scores of ministers sitting at their feet to be initiated in their new doctrine, retired altogether from the movement after this, and for some little time nothing was heard of it.

Presently *The Life of Faith* was started, and the statements were at first very carefully guarded. By degrees, meetings were again held, and the nomenclature was modified. They were convened for "the deepening of the spiritual life," and other such apparently desirable objects. But the language has been gradually getting more "unguarded," and some of the speakers on this new platform have now too often to explain what they do not mean: and that they do not *go as far* as some others who are more advanced.

THE INDICTMENT OF THE MODERN MOVEMENT

But our indictment of the whole movement is this:

(1) ITS PROMOTERS SUBSTITUTE "FAITH" FOR "HOPE"; THAT IS THEY SUBSTITUTE MAN'S METHOD FOR GOD'S.

It is the Romish expression, "an act of faith" which is to accomplish some sudden change. Everywhere this is insisted upon.

(2) ORIGINATING IN ITSELF.

The whole movement commences with *self*, and *self* is the one great object all through. True, it is so veiled, that it is calculated to deceive the very elect. Self is ever before the mind. However much the Holy Spirit or Christ may be mentioned, the one object is *my spiritual life*. How this is to be deepened or heightened or increased, is the one great subject, whatever may be the title of the address or of the book. It all comes to this, that it must begin with *self.*

- o "It has to do with the personal will of each individual."[1]
- o "You are waiting for the fire, and it will come when you have yielded that which is in debate between you and your God."[2]

In the first instance, everything depends on *one's self.* Certain "conditions must be fulfilled."

(1.) The first is presented thus:

- o "Be cleansed from all sin of which you may be conscious . . . The cleansed heart is an essential condition of spirit filling."[3]

------

[1] *The Christian,* Oct. 24, 1895, p. 10.

[2] *The Keswick Week,* 1895, p. 27.

[3] *A Keswick Experience,* by F. B. Meyer, p. 14.

(2.) Then having got this cleansed heart "the Holy Spirit is within your reach.[4]

(3.) But even when filled it is of no use

- o "To live in a very ocean of power and love, if we are unable to discern its presence, or appropriate its marvelous properties."

- o "These conditions must be fulfilled before you can exercise that faith and receive that supreme gift."[5]

(3) SELF-EXALTING.

Thus, *self* is at the very outset exalted. Indeed, it is practically almighty. Doubtless, it is repeated again and again by speakers and writers, that God must do all, and that the Spirit must fill, and Christ must cleanse. All this is very properly insisted upon. But there is a *preliminary act* of *self* which is superior to all, and this is insisted on in spite of

---

[4] *ibid,* p. 13.
[5] *Ibid,* p. 14.

Christ's words, "Without ME ye can do NOTHING." But if anyone could possibly perform this greatest and most difficult, and most important act of all, then he requires nothing more. If he can do *that*, he can surely do all the rest, for all else is simple compared with it. And yet the language employed does not recognise the supremacy and sovereignty of God.

He is exhorted thus:

- o "Let Him have His way with you."[6]
- o "The process of dying, in the awful act of baptism, which *may* take place (God knows) at the time of the physical placing in the water, or not; but it *must* take place sometime by the soul's free will, by the man's determination, by the surrender of self, the flesh, and the world, unto God, in Jesus Christ our Lord."[7]
- o "Let the Holy Spirit of God come with the condemnation of sin and the Cross of Christ.

———————————————

[6] *The Keswick Week,* 1895, p. 36.
[7] *Ibid.* p. 88.

Give over the flesh to death, and the Spirit of God will come in."[8]

o "God is waiting, Christ is waiting, the Holy Ghost is waiting."[9]

o "Open your heart tonight and be filled with the Spirit."[10]

o "Let us learn to have Him for our sanctification, not only in theory, but in fact."[11]

o "God will now be able to use you."[12]

o "Let Jesus have His way with you."[13]

o "Come tonight and make yourselves ready; prepare yourselves for that word 'We can.' That is consecration."[14]

o "Oh, become willing to bow before God in conviction and confession!"[15]

---

[8] *Ibid.* p. 49.

[9] *Ibid.* p. 53.

[10] *Ibid.* p. 54.

[11] *Ibid.* p. 65.

[12] *Ibid.* p. 76.

[13] *The Keswick Week,* 1895, p. 76.

[14] *Ibid.* p. 79.

[15] *Ibid.* p. 52

Now these are by no means either the words or the teaching of Scripture. It is written "It is GOD that worketh in YOU both TO WILL and TO DO of His good pleasure" (Phil. 2:13). Unless God first works it IN, in vain shall any seek to work it OUT. So also, as to the gifts and graces of the Holy Spirit it is written, "All these worketh that one and the selfsame Spirit, dividing to every man severally AS HE WILL" (1 Cor. 12:11), not as we will.

This is quite opposed to the God-dishonouring expressions which practically exalt the creature above the Creator, when we are told to LET God "do this"; "ALLOW the Holy Spirit" to do that; and "ENABLE Christ" to do the other. This is the language which pervades the new movement, to say nothing of such expressions as: "God cannot give us the fruits of the Spirit without the congenial atmosphere."[16]

Such language not only everywhere characterises this teaching but is the very essence of it.

---

[16] *The Christian,* October 24, 1895, p. 10.

But it is not the language of Holy Scripture! This declares that all who are "in Christ" are new creations, that they died with Christ, and "have been crucified with Christ." These teachers, on the other hand, represent that believers have got *to crucify themselves now*. One of them quotes this very passage: "I am crucified with Christ: nevertheless, I live"; and he asks, "what does he (the apostle) mean?" "He means that he *has put self on the cross* . . . that it may be crucified."[17]

This is stated, unmindful of the fact that while Romans is *doctrinal*, Galatians 2:20 is *subjective*. The Greek is, "I HAVE BEEN crucified with Christ"; *i.e.* when Christ was crucified, God viewed my old nature as having been crucified with Christ, which agrees with that other past tense in Rom. 6:6, "Our old man WAS crucified with Him." There is not a word about Paul or anyone else crucifying themselves; and, indeed, it would puzzle anyone to explain how it could possibly be done. If God did not see His people crucified in and with Christ when He hung upon

---

[17] *The Keswick*, 1895, p. 85.

The Road to Holiness 21

the cross; if the members of Christ's Body were not reckoned by God as having been then crucified with the Head of that Body, then at no time since could it ever be done. It is too late for anyone to attempt the task which is talked so lightly about.

Another says:

- o "Only yield yourselves to God and let Him have His way with you and you and I too shall feel tonight, it may be, the touch of this Pentecostal fire until we are severed from ourselves forever; and it shall be said, 'These men have been with Jesus, they are new men.' The old creation has passed away; behold, all is become new."[18]

Such language as this argues an utter ignorance of the salvation wherewith God has saved His people, and of what He has made Christ to be to them, and what He has made them to be in Christ and fails to recognise the great distinction between

---

[18] *The Keswick Week,* 1895, p. 36.

the similarity of grace given to all believers, and the diversity of their gifts.

Another says:

- o "What is this crucifixion of self? It has to do with the personal will of each individual. It is more than renunciation; you have been renouncing your sins at every conference you have attended. Without this crucifixion and death of self-there can be no coming in of the new life. My responsibility is in the yielding and consenting to that death . . . But are you prepared to consent to this death, in order that you may have the cleansing of the Spirit, and the anointing of the Spirit for service?"[19]

Here, again, we have man practically almighty, and addressed as though he were able to perform the most difficult and important work of all, in order that the primary condition may be fulfilled.

---

[19] *The Christian*, Oct. 24, 1895, p. 10.

(4) "ANOTHER SPIRIT."

The whole system of teaching subverts the work, and mission, and office of the Holy Spirit.

It has often been well said, that the work of the Holy Ghost is not to direct our attention to *His work in us*, but to *Christ's work for us*. This is absolutely true. "HE SHALL GLORIFY ME," was Christ's own definition of that which characterises the work of the Holy Spirit.

But Keswick teaching is the very opposite of this. It places the Lord Jesus in an inferior position to the Holy Spirit, and thereby contradicts the teaching of that same Blessed Spirit when He declares that Christ is "all in all," and that His mission is to glorify Christ. It occupies me wholly with the work of the Spirit *in* me and *through me*. I am to be filled with the Spirit. I am exhorted to "claim and receive it by an act of faith": or, as another has put it, "The all-engrossing theme of *how to receive the Pentecostal gift.*"[20]

---

[20] *A Keswick Experience*, p. 4.

If I could fulfil all the conditions which are laid down for me, and obey all the "rules for daily living" which are prescribed, I should have every reason to glorify myself, but I should, at the same time, have the evidence that it is the working of "another Spirit" (2 Cor. 11:4); for of the Holy Spirit it is declared that His work is known by His abasing man, and glorifying and exalting Christ (1 Cor. 1:31). When He works in us, Christ is not a mere helper, or a makeweight, or a puppet, in my hands, but my all in all, occupying my thoughts, filling my heart, and unconsciously influencing my life. This is the only evidence of the Holy Spirit's presence and power.

(5) THE TWO NATURES[21] DENIED.

The Keswick teaching has its own terminology, and thus proves itself to be *new*. But it has been well said, "what is true is not new, and what is new is not true."

---

[21] For more on this see E. W. Bullinger's *The Two Natures in the Child of God*, published by The Open Bible Trust – details at the end of this book.

- "A cleansed heart" is one of their commonest expressions.

- "The baptism of the Holy Ghost means just the cleansing of the heart from all unrighteousness, then a filling of the Spirit."[22]
- "Sanctification begins at the heart, though it does not end there."[23]
- "You must get the heart right, or nothing will be right."[24]
- This "clean" or "cleansed heart" is one of their commonest expressions. But the question is, *which heart?*

Scripture speaks of two natures – the "old" and the "new." Which of these two is meant when such language is used?

---

[22] *The Christian*, Oct. 24, 1895, p. 11.
[23] *The Keswick Week*, 1895, p. 25.
[24] *The Keswick Week*, 1895, p. 25.

If it be the "old" nature, then *nothing can ever cleanse it*! God has declared that it is "desperately wicked," and impossible of renovation. "Who can bring a clean thing out of an unclean? Not one." (Job 14:4). And Christ declares that all evil springs from this old heart. (Matt. 15:16-20.)

And if it be the "new" nature, it *needs no cleansing.* The old heart or nature has been thoroughly judged and condemned by God; and for His people it has been crucified with Christ. The NEW heart or nature CANNOT sin, for it is born of God. (1 Jn 3:9.)

Their diverse nature is declared in John 3:8 – "That which is born of the flesh is flesh, and that which is born of the Spirit is spirit." And their hostility is declared in Gal. 5:17 – "These are contrary the one to the other." (See also Rom. 7:23; 8:6, 7.) The flesh is never changed into spirit, and the spirit can never be changed into flesh.

The Keswick teaching, therefore, at the very outset, by talking of the "*cleansed heart*," perverts the great foundation of the Christian position, and denies the central truth of our Christian standing. And owing to the denial by some and the criminal silence observed by others as to the doctrine and truth of the TWO NATURES in the believer, Satan has filled up the vacuum thus left, with the results which we deplore.

(6) SCRIPTURE MISAPPLIED.

The way in which Scripture is dealt with is also very strained, forced and novel. The Bible Reading in *The Keswick Week*, 1895, pp. 32-37, is a gross parody of one of the most solemn dispensational chapters of the Old Testament, viz. Isaiah 6. And to say the least, a most sacred Scripture is touched with a very irreverent hand.

In some of the smaller books there is scarcely a reference to the Word of God and even then, it is often misquoted. That important verse, 2 Cor. 3:18, "We beholding ARE changed into the same image," for example, in *The Keswick Week*, 1895, p. 30, is given, "May be changed." The speaker knows best why he thus misquotes it. In another little book we are told to behold and then "try and be changed."

Then again, forced, not to say wrong applications are made altogether, such as the address on 1 Cor. 3, in *The Keswick Week,* 1895, pp. 48, etc. The whole point of the interpretation is missed, and quite a different use is made of the passage from that for which it was given.

Too often, also, those who are "in Christ" are sent back to the Old Testament and placed on old covenant ground, as is done when the Christian position is drawn from Psalm 51 instead of from Romans 8.[25]

(7) A NEW TERMINOLOGY IS INTRODUCED ...

... to suit the new doctrines. This is not surprising, but rather, inevitable. Phrases such as "claiming a second blessing," "claiming a full salvation,"

---

[25] See the latest work of Rev. Andrew Murray on Ps. 51.

"absolute surrender," "a consecrated man," "the clean heart," "redeeming Spirit," "Pentecostal fire" and "Pentecostal enduement" (truly only gifts, not of grace), these are the outcome of the new Theology.

These have taken the place of the spiritual language, of "growing in grace," "walking worthy of our vocation," etc., etc.

Even *truth* is put out of all proportion and such a term as "Consecration," of which we read nothing in the New Testament and very little in the Old Testament (on the part of man) is used with such frequency as practically to usurp the place of all other truth.

(8) IRREVERENT LANGUAGE ...

... perhaps, is too common on all hands for much to be thought of it; otherwise there is an abundance of this, such as:

- o "Take God back with you."[26]
- o An "Easter Jesus."[27]
- o "A smell of Pentecostal fire," etc. etc.[28]

(9) CHRIST'S NATURE AND WORK DISHONOURED.

We have lately seen, in *The Holiest of All,* how absolutely false doctrine concerning the Person of our Lord can be tolerated and excused.

One of their most prominent spokesmen teaches and declares that Christ partook of our "fallen nature" and that though He was "sinless" in that He did not *yield* to sin and commit sin, yet that He had our fallen nature within Him to contend with.

Mr. Murray has since disclaimed this[29] to the extent that for "fallen nature" he proposes to

---

[26] *The Keswick Week,* 1895, p. 22.

[27] *Ibid.* p. 35.

[28] *Ibid.* p. 35.

[29] See *The Christian,* Nov. 7, 1895; and *The Life of Faith,* Nov. 6, 1895.

substitute, in a new edition, "our human nature." But "our human nature" IS "fallen nature," so that the distinction in words does not seem to make much difference in fact. Indeed, the following extracts are altogether inconsistent with the inherent perfection or sinlessness of Christ's nature. It comes to exactly the same thing; for whatever may be the terms employed, the teaching based upon them is one and the same.

How can the term "fallen nature" be limited to the mere weaknesses and "liability to weariness," etc. of Christ as man, in the fact of the following quotations?

o "As nothing but the eternal Spirit could have overcome or redeemed fallen nature – *as Christ took it upon Him* – so nothing can possibly overcome or redeem the fallen soul or body of any child of Adam but that same overcoming and *redeeming Spirit* really living and acting in it, IN THE SAME MANNER AS IT DID IN THE HUMANITY OF CHRIST"! (p. 305.)

According to this it is not "the blood of Christ" which redeems fallen nature, but the "redeeming Spirit"; and Christ Himself needed this "redeeming Spirit"; therefore, He needed a sacrifice, and like Aaron, "by reason hereof He ought, as for the people so also for Himself, to offer for sins." (Heb. 5:3.)

Again, Mr. Murray says of Christ that;

- o "He had to fast and watch and pray *lest the lawful desire of His human nature might lead to sin;* THUS, HE WAS PERFECTED. And this is Christian perfection – the fellowship with Christ through the indwelling Spirit in His obedience." (p. 201.)

It is vain for Mr. Murray to disclaim the words "fallen nature," when this is his belief, and this is his teaching based upon it.

It is not a question of terminology, but of theology; and the aim and design and effect of his book cannot be altered by the mere change of an expression.

Examples of this false doctrine have already been given,[30] but we may well add a few more.

EXTRACTS FROM *THE HOLIEST OF ALL.*[31]

1."Out of each victory He came with His will STRENGTHENED, and *His power over the weakness of the flesh, and the danger of yielding to its desire,* for earthly good, or its fear of temporal evil, INCREASED." (p. 185.)

2. "By not doing His own will, but the will of the Father, by the sacrifice of Himself to God and His will, He conquered sin *in His own person* and gained a victory over it, whereby it was forever vanquished and brought to nought. (p. 325.)

------

[30] See *Things to Come*, Oct. 1895.
[31] By the Rev. Andrew Murray. The *italics, etc.* in quotations are ours.

3. "As it was through the Spirit that God wrought that perfect work in Christ by which *fallen human nature as He had taken it upon Himself* was redeemed and glorified, so nothing can make us partakers of that redeeming and quickening power but that same Spirit, truly living and working in our soul and body, IN THE SAME MANNER AS IT DID IN THE HUMANITY OF CHRIST." (p. 540.)

4. "Let the cleansing of sins be to you, *as it was to Christ* the entrance to the Holiest." (pp. 45, 46.)

5. "In the Incarnation the union between the divine and the human nature was only begun: *it had to be perfected by Christ, in His human will, yielding Himself to God's will*, even unto death." (p. 52.)

6. "*He hath perfected them forever.*" "The perfection *in both cases is one and the same*. As the Son of man, as the second Adam, who lives in all who are His, He perfected Himself for them, and them in Himself *His perfection and theirs is one*," *i.e.* here below on earth! (p. 345.)

7. "Jesus denied Himself, would do nothing to please that nature He had taken, sinless though it was in Him. *He denied it, He died to it. This was to Him the path of life."* (p. 364.)

FROM *THE LIFE OF FAITH.*[32]

8. "The natural life which Jesus had from his mother – that natural life in connection with Adam and with us in the flesh – *He gave it up to death, the accursed death of Calvary.* Christ said then in effect, *O Father spare not . . ..* I tell you, you must surrender everything *as accursed.* People won't believe that everything *in our nature is under the curse;* and yet it is so." (p. 398.)

It is impossible for Mr. Murray to use language like this and yet be credited with a belief in the inherent sinless perfection of Christ's human nature. How can that which is already perfect be *"perfected," "strengthened,"* or *"increased"*? And besides, observe in these statements that in No. 7 the word *"sinless"* must mean that He kept

---

[32] July 31, 18965

Himself from sinning and so He *denied His nature* and *died to it,"* as being an *"accursed thing."* "He gave it up to death, *the accursed death of Calvary,"* "and said in effect, O Father spare not." Is this Christianity? We always thought that Christ died under the curse of the law AS A SUBSTITUTE for those who had broken the law according to the Apostle's argument (Gal. 3:10, 13). But we never before heard that it was because His own nature was under the curse, and that for this reason, on Calvary He "said in effect, O Father spare not." If this is truth, or like Christian truth, the painful question arises as to what blasphemy against Christ our Lord would be?

This doctrine has, so far, passed unrebuked and un-condemned (at any rate, publicly) by the leaders of the Holiness movement, and therefore they are partakers of the evil.

Failing to get man up to the perfection of the Christ of God and the Christ of the Scriptures, they would fain drag Christ down, so that man may be the more easily exalted to His level!

Hence it is that Christ, the spotless holy Lamb of God, is said to have taken our "fallen nature" upon Him.

But other speakers on the Keswick platform use language almost as bad – and coming perilously near to such a dishonour of Christ, one of them, speaking of Christ's death, says:

- o "Sin took Him there. But if we say that He died *through* sin and for sin, we have by no means exhausted the deep meaning of the expression; for it also means that He died *so as to have done with sin forever*, in all its possible relations *to Himself*. He died so as to have done with the *penalty of sin* so as to have done with *the guilt* which He incurred voluntarily as to our representative; He died so as to have done with the *power of sin*, so that it could no longer press upon His soul and make Him feel that the *Father* had forsaken Him, because He was the representative of sin on our behalf; He died so as to have done with the contact and with the pressure upon His *own soul of sin*, for He had through His life upon earth endured the contradiction of sinners and felt the pressure of agony, from the presence and *potent influence of sin upon* Him, until at last He sweated great drops of blood, in the Garden of Gethsemane; and on the cross He cried 'My God! My God! why has Thou forsaken Me?' Christ Jesus died so as to cease from all penalty, all guilt, all power, all contact, all *influence* of sin and He started forth from that moment perfectly *free* in every possible sense *from sin,* in all its bearings, all its connections, all its meanings, and in all its powers."[33]

Again, in a subsequent address, the same speaker says:

o "Look at the Lord Jesus Christ in His manhood, learning *to crucify self, so as to give up His will* to God; for, remember, He had a distinct *will* as Man; He had the power of using His free will *exactly as any other*

---

[33] *The Keswick Week,* 1895, p. 40.

man has. Adam was meant to be the perfect representative of humanity, as God would have it. Christ, as the second Man from heaven, must do what Adam failed to do – *He must consecrate* His will to God; and in that sense He must *let it be crucified.* He had to say, 'Not My will, but Thine be done'; and this was crucifixion of the will. It was the Person of Christ – the *ego*, the *I* – giving Himself over to His God and Father, though it cost Him crucifixion. It was giving up self to the place of death, that He might bring *a perfected humanity* through death into life, and thus as Man, become one with God forever.

o "Secondly, He had to *crucify the flesh*, quite irrespective now of the atonement or propitiation. I am speaking of Him as Man. He had to crucify the flesh *with its affections;* not its lusts in a bad sense, because His appetites and tastes were perfectly pure. He was 'harmless, undefiled and separate from sinners.' *But He had his tastes and desires and these He had to crucify*. He gave His very nature, with all its tastes and appetites, which were human, though pure and spotless, to be crucified, in order again that He might

- "PRESENT A PERFECT MAN TO GOD THE FATHER."[34]

Now, to say the least, such language is a wicked libel on the Holy one of God. He *did* have "His tastes and desires," and they were perfect. They were the manifestations of God's affections and were always well-pleasing to the Father! To assert that they had to be *crucified* is a jumble of nonsense and blasphemy and this one sentence, spoken at Keswick in 1895 by one of their most prominent speakers, ought to open the eyes of all, and fill the souls of all true Christians with righteous anger. Were Christ's affections, tastes and appetites wrong or unlawful? He loved, He pitied, He wept. Had these "affections" to be crucified? Why, they are the very things that charm the heart and call forth the love of His

---

[34] *Keswick Week*, 1895, p. 84. The *italics* are ours.

people, as they did the good-pleasure of the Father!

Another speaker said of the blessed Lord Jesus, still more unscripturally:

- o "Gethsemane means the surrender of the will. That is the cup. *It cost Him a struggle* to say, in other words, 'Thy will shall be done, I will drink it up'; but He conquered."[35]

CHRIST LOWERED THAT MAN MAY BE RAISED.

But why this desire to lower the Lord Jesus? Let them explain, as the same speaker afterwards does. All that is thus said of Christ, is only to emphasise the great lesson for which the foundation has thus been laid in order to teach;

- o "That exactly as the Lord Jesus Christ crucified self, and took self to death, so men

---

[35] *The Keswick Week*, 1895. p. 78.

must, *before they can really receive the full benefit of Christ's salvation bring self to the cross and die.* They must die as Christ died. It may be a long process, as St. Paul said, 'I am crucified with Christ: nevertheless, I live.' What does he mean? He means that he has put self on the cross. He does not say, 'Self is dead,' though that is true judicially. But morally, experimentally – subjectively, as we call it – he has put self on to the cross that it may be crucified. It is bound where Christ was bound, and the nails can never be taken out till the action of death is fulfilled. And the Lord Jesus Christ having done this for us, faith says, by the grace of God by the power of the Holy Ghost, I take my place in His death and give self to be crucified, exactly as Christ did for my sake."[36]

It is difficult to recognise, here, the old-fashioned doctrines of the Reformation! Where is the Word of God in all this? There is scarcely one passage that is rightly interpreted or applied. We have

---

[36] *The Keswick Week,* 1895, p. 85.

already pointed out that the words of Gal. 2:20, should be (and are in the R.V.) rendered, "I HAVE BEEN crucified with Christ." In the Epistle to the Romans we have the objective judicial aspect of this wondrous fact; while in Gal. 2:20 we have the statement of the Apostle's *personal* and *subjective* application of the Christian revelation and the secret of *his* life as a Christian and an Apostle. It is a glorious summing up of *his* faith, the mainspring of his wonderful activity.

(10) THE MEASURE OF THE PERFECTION.

But besides this very questionable doctrine, which so gravely affects the adorable person of our blessed Lord, lowering Him from His high and holy position, there are other statements which affect the undue exaltation of man, even of the believer.

One speaker says:

- o "Until the soul is prepared by this cleansing of the Spirit, there cannot be that perfectness and likeness to Christ *which is possible for us all.*"[37]

Speaking of "the law of the mind" and "the law of sin," in Rom. 7 the same speaker said:

- o "Is there deliverance from this law? I am here to say, not merely as an advocate, but as a witness, that there *is deliverance*, and that there may come upon every soul that anointing of the Spirit of God, because there may come to every soul this cleansing of the Spirit of God."[38]

This is the speaker who further on uses the words already quoted, to show that this cleansing rest with ourselves.

But where is the new doctrine about this *"cleansing of the Spirit"* to be found in the Word of God? *There* we have always read that we are *cleansed* only "by the blood of Christ," in His

---

[37] *The Christian*, Oct. 24, 1895, p. 10.
[38] *The Christian,* Oct. 24, 1895, p. 10.

atoning death. But little is heard of atonement or of justification, with all their attendant blessings, in the language of these speakers.

Another speaker said:

- o It is not a life of passivity, but of intense activity. *I now live a life with Him of perpetual faith.*"[39]

Another speaker said:

- o "If you learn to bless the Lord at all times, you must find out *the secret of perpetual victory over sin.*"[40]

Another writer says:

- o "The way into the Holiest is the living way of *perfect conformity to Jesus, wrought in us by His Spirit.*"[41]

---

[39] *The Keswick Week*, 1895, p. 31.
[40] *Ibid.* p. 97.
[41] *The Holies of All*, p. 364.

This language, of course, falls far short of that which is employed by those who have advanced further down this dangerous road.

This brings us to another point, and that is that the whole of this new movement is:

(11) AN INCLINED PLANE.

It must be admitted that most of the Keswick speakers disclaim that to which such language as the above leads. But surely there must be something very wrong, when one so often hears of regrets from some speakers about the "unguarded" (that is their term) language of others! What is there which makes it so necessary for their speakers to be on their guard? There must be some unexplained danger in that *inclined plane* which commences with such apparent harmlessness!
Ritualism is often pointed at, judged and condemned as being so dangerous because of the fact that Rome is its logical end. Even so is the danger of this "Holiness movement" to be known, judged and condemned with equal clearness; for, commencing with merely a deepening of the

spiritual life, its only logical terminus is the *Agapemone*!

We are not speaking unadvisedly. The modern holiness movement is *an inclined plane*. The various speakers are at different places upon that plane. Some are nearer the upper end; some are further down; some are nearer the lower end, while others are lying as wrecks at the bottom.

Some are so far down that they are not allowed upon the Keswick platform. A line is thus drawn, and all below and beyond that line is marked "dangerous."

Those who are on this *dangerous* ground are not slow to see and point out the manifest inconsistency of this. They can see that the position of their Keswick friends is most illogical; for while the premises of both parties are the same, the conclusions of the more advanced party are the more logical. Hence the Editor of the *Tongues of*

Fire[42] very pointedly says of these two parties, those above and those below the line:

- o "Perhaps instead of calling them two schools, we should describe one [*i.e.* the Keswick party] *as a preliminary seminary*, the other as *God's Holy Ghost College (!)* ... These teachers tell us that the best thing God can or will do with is sin is to subdue it, to repress it somewhere in the believer. They agree that in heaven we are to be pure and holy, but that Almighty God must enlist the help of death before sin can be entirely removed. One of the most prominent of these teachers, a worthy Prebendary in the Church of England, recently *stated*, in the most public manner, that sin must indwell us to the last moment of our lives, adding:

- o "'When I read such words as dear John Wesley's. "The evil root the carnal mind, is destroyed in me; sin subsists no longer." I can only marvel that any human being with

---

[42] Nov. 1895, p. 2. Italics ours.

the teaching of the Holy Ghost upon the Word of God, can thus deceive himself or attempt to deceive others. It is, I think, a miracle of blindness that we can study God's Word and imagine that any man can be free from sin experimentally while here in the mortal body.'[43]

o "It is refreshing to remember that this so-called 'miracle of blindness' was used of God to found the largest English-speaking Church in the world, and that his followers today number between twenty and thirty million."

o "It is clear, however, that the
   "REPRESSIVE PREBENDARY"
   and his friends belonging to *the preliminary seminary*, hold that sin must remain in the believer until death delivers him. Upon this we would like to ask a few plain questions."

---

[43] *The Keswick Week*, 1895. p. 39.

Instead of troubling our readers with these questions, it will be sufficient to quote another editorial in the same issue of *Tongues of Fire* (page 1):

"AN OFFER TO THE KESWICK PLATFORM."

"In consequence of the public statement made by the Rev. Prebendary Webb-Peploe at the recent Keswick Convention and published in *The Keswick Week* (the official report of that Convention, edited by the Rev. Evan H. Hopkins), that sin must remain in the cleansed and Spirit-filled believer until death, and that all who truly represent themselves as Keswick speakers so teach, we make the following offer.

"The editor of *Tongues of Fire* will pay the sum of £100 (for the benefit of the Keswick Mission Fund) to the first Keswick speaker who forwards him a passage of Scripture which, read with the context, positively affirms the necessity of sin in the Spirit-filled believer.

"We will publish in our December number the response (if any) which we may receive to this offer.

"We are sure that Mr. Webb-Peploe's statement did not meet with the approval of the vast majority of those attending the Keswick Convention. It was made. It has not been withdrawn. Hence our offer."

In *The Christian* (Nov. 14, 1895) we are thankful to see a protest entered against the above quotations and the "Controversial Methods" of Mr. Reader Harris.

It is perfectly evident therefore that there are leaders in this modern Holiness movement who are far in advance of the Keswick teachers, and who would not be tolerated on the Keswick platform. Why is this? It is because they are, as we have said all on an inclined plane and those who occupy the lowest place upon it are the most logical.

But our point is, that both are alike wrong. The very *premises* of both parties are wrong, and hence their conclusions also are wrong. The only difference is that those in the "preliminary seminary" are not so logical in their conclusions as those in the more advanced and irreverently-named "College"; and are not able to answer or contend with them.

Now it is a fact which cannot be doubted or denied, that the more anyone applies himself to any profession, art, business, or study, the more he excels in it. The more thoroughly he follows and carries out any true principle of action, the more nearly he advances to the goal to which he aspires. But with the modern Holiness movement, all this is reversed. It appears from the protest of *The Christian* against the teaching of the *Tongues of Fire*, that it is possible to go too far. It is evident that the more perfectly anyone carries out the Keswick teaching, the more dangerous is the ground on which he treads. The more thoroughly he fulfils the "conditions" laid down, the nearer he approaches to error. And the further he advances in that error, the nearer he approaches to the *Agapemone*, which has already received some of the victims who, with some others, *began* by simply trying to deepen their spiritual life, and now lie at the bottom of that inclined plane, wrecked and ruined.

It must not be answered that every movement has amongst its promoters those who have brought discredit upon it. This is only true where such persons have acted contrary to the principles on which the movement is based. But in this case, those who have thus made shipwreck have done so in *consequence* of those principles, not in spite of them. They have simply been more consistent in acting on the principles taught; more faithful in complying with the "conditions" laid down; and more logical in carrying them to their legitimate conclusion.

Some of the leaders of the movement are probably among those who abstain from alcoholic drinks, simply because of the fact that drunkenness is the possible, yea probable, end. Hence, they condemn the "moderate drinker" without reserve, because he is, they urge, on an inclined plane! How strange that the working of the principle can be seen so plainly in the one case and their eyes be blinded to the other all the time! There is something which is more awful than drunkenness in the sight of God, and that is the condition of those who, He says, are *"Drunk, but not with wine."*

(12) WHAT IT CAN TOLERATE.

There is little that is read in their Holiness books or heard on their platforms that Roman Catholics could not say or listen to! And Keswick teaching is, moreover, quite compatible with genuflections, and an advanced Ritual. It unites all Armenians' and Semi-Pelagians; and amongst its prominent teachers may be found those who have musical services, adopt the "Pleasant Sunday Afternoon" amusements and surplice choirs; who can use *Hymns Ancient and Modern* and can take part with Down-grade ministers in the new Socialistic movement of "Citizen Sunday"! There must be something radically wrong where such a latitude of toleration is possible.

(13) THE MOVEMENT A FAILURE.

But this brings us to the last point and the great fact that we see little or *no difference* in those who hold the Keswick doctrines! – whether in the "Seminary" or the "College." They are like all other Christians. They have the same old nature, they have the same flesh within them; and we see the same tempers, the same self-assertion, the same spiritual pride, yea, the same sins in them as in others. *The Christian* (Nov. 14, 1895) well points out this fact in the case of Mr. Reader Harris, referred to on p. 20.

And we often see a more advanced holiness of life, and a greater separation from the world, in many who have kept quite aloof from the new movement. For there were saints of God who enjoyed a deeper spiritual life, and manifested a holier spiritual walk, before Mr. and Mrs. Pearsall Smith were born, or a house in Keswick was built.

THE FAILURE ADMITTED

And finally, as a movement, its failure is admitted. It fails to accomplish the object sought for. It is mournfully confessed that the "blessing," so-called may be lost; that there are sad "alternations" in these "emotional" exercises. One of their speakers asserts that:

- o "There are hundreds at every Convention who learn new truth and experience new joy and make new vows of loyalty, but it is;

"ALL GONE IN A MOMENT"[44]

Another speaks of:

- o "Christians who sometimes get a blessing and lose it again."[45]

---

[44] *The Keswick Week*, 1895, p. 14. Capital letters and line theirs.
[45] *Ibid.* p. 48.

Another speaker utters his lamentation and says:

- o "What might not happen in the religious history of our great City if every soul present, before the meeting closed, were to receive, some for the first time, others, perhaps, FOR THE HUNDRETH TIME, the enduement of the Holy Ghost as a power for service!"[46]

Another speaker said:

- o "We meet together to ask God to strengthen us and to encourage and strengthen one another in being maintained in the position of the spiritual Christ. It is

  "SO EASY TO GO BACK"

  in our walk and experience, to the flesh. We need every help one can get in order that having begun to live a life in the fulness of

---

[46] *The Christian*, October 24th, 1895, p. 10.

the Spirit we should never go back again to a lower level, to a fleshly walk."[47]

No wonder we are beginning to hear already of meetings for "*Re-Consecration.*" True, these are in connection with the Salvation Army, which like "the Pentecostal League," carries the same principles, we must confess. to a more logical conclusion; but the fact testifies to failure.

In the face of this failure we would fain urge upon the Lord's people:

"A MORE EXCELLENT WAY."

Of course, there is some truth mixed up in all this. It would be strange indeed were it not so. It is not *all* error. We all desire the same conformity to Christ, the same separation from the world, the same graces and gifts which God has treasured up in the glorious Head in heaven, for the supply of the members of His Body here upon earth.

---

[47] *The Keswick Week*, 1895, pp. 64, 65. Capital letters, and line theirs.

But it is here that we join issue with many of our brethren. Not with their *end*, but with their *means*. We would say to them and to all who are perplexed by their teaching. What you desire is right, but you go the wrong way to get it. There is a way more honouring to God, more easy, more simple, more efficacious – in short,

"A MORE EXCELLENT WAY,"

simply because it is God's way.

"Which of you, by taking thought, can add one cubit unto his stature?" (Matt. 6:27).

This is a very important question and can be very pertinently applied to the whole Keswick movement. You are all "taking thought" to add to, to heighten, or deepen your spiritual "stature." But the Saviour's words remind us of the Laws of nature and show us that "stature" is not to be added to by such means, for the means used must correspond with the end to be reached. Given the means of proper nourishment and pure air, stature *must* increase unconsciously and without an effort. Nay, it cannot be repressed! When we use the means of eating and breathing, the *end* is not ever before our minds as an *object*, but we enjoy the means which secure the end. So, it must be with our spiritual stature. "Christ is our life" – and the mission of the Holy Spirit is to take of the things of Christ and minister them unto us. We feed upon Christ in His death, as in eating and drinking (John 6:48-63), and our spiritual stature is added to without "taking thought." The Blesser becomes our object and "all blessings" are ours in Him. (Eph. 1:3) The Blesser is our object and not "the blessing." The blessing is ensured and secured in Him.

It is the work of the Holy Spirit to witness in our hearts of Christ, but the great tendency of Keswick teaching, as we have seen, is to occupy us with the Spirit's witness *within* us, instead of with Christ's work *for* us, of whom and which He witnesses. Hence, we are occupied with the *means* and miss the *end*, while we lose the very blessing which we seek. Hence, the failure which is admitted and mourned over.

THE AIM OF THE ENEMY

And our great enemy is all the while well content. He knows (if Christians do not) that Christ is the source of all our strength and blessing. His one aim, therefore, is to keep the heart from being occupied with Christ. Any means will serve his purpose so long as this can be accomplished. Hence, he will occupy;

> The sinner with his sins,
> The penitent with his repentance,
> The believer with his faith,
> The servant with his service, and
> The saint with his holiness.

Anything, so long as it is not Christ. This is the great blot on this *modern* movement. And it is certain that many souls are perplexed and hindered by thus being directed to *self-occupation*.

The whole system of teaching is calculated to centre the thoughts and the attention on self, however much the Holy Spirit and Christ may be mentioned.

It all begins with self and the "conditions" which self must fulfil. It is all summed up in the significant words "if" and "we."

The "more excellent way" is laid down for us in:

2 Corinthians 3:18.

"We, beholding-as-in-a-mirror the glory of the Lord, ARE CHANGED into the same image from glory to glory even as by the Spirit of the Lord."

The point is this. Moses, when he went up into the mount, saw the glory of the Lord and when he came down his face shone with the reflection of it.

From 1 John 3:1-3 we learn that the *actual* sight of the Lord Jesus will make us really like Him in body, as well as in soul and spirit. Even so now, it is as we behold Him with the eye of faith, that we are transformed into His likeness. If we are *occupied* with Christ we necessarily have a deeper realization of Christ and hence cannot but unconsciously reflect His glory. If we are occupied with a heavenly object, we shall become heavenly, our countenances, our walk, our life, will shine. *We* may not see it; we may not know it: we may be quite unconscious of it. Moses saw not his own countenance, but the people saw it. So, it will be with us. It is not some standard which we have got to reach; it is not some emotion which we have got to feel; it is not some "blessing" which we have got to "claim"; it is not some "act of faith," or "act of surrender," or any "act" of our own, but it is simply the occupation of the heart with Christ in glory and not with the Holy Spirit: with Calvary and not with Pentecost!

The great work of the Holy Spirit is to glorify Christ, and the best evidence we can possibly have that we are "filled with the Spirit" is this – that we are occupied with Christ. In other words, *the measure in which we are filled with the Spirit is to be known by the measure in which our hearts are filled up and taken up with Christ*; and the test of this is not the excitement of any emotional feelings, but a readiness to receive and to be guided by ALL the teaching of God's holy Word.

If we be not wholly occupied and satisfied with Christ, then truly it is "another Jesus" that is being preached; "another spirit" which has been received; and "another gospel" which has been accepted (2 Cor. 11:3, 4). It is an awful fact that there are *other spirits* which may energize the old nature and hence the solemn warnings to be on our guard against them and to "try" or prove them (1 Tim. 4:1; 1 Cor. 14:29; 1 John 4:1, etc.).

Now, see how the "will of God" is manifested in securing our sanctification. "Looking off unto Jesus" is the simple means to this great end, and to ensure that His people shall be looking TO Christ, God has given us the "blessed hope" of looking FOR Christ. Hence this has been well called "the purifying hope" (1 John 3:1-3).

If Conferences are to be held at all, then those for the Study of Truth connected with the Lord's Coming, are much more calculated to

produce holiness of life, than those convened especially for that purpose.

We may well apply:

JEHOVAH'S SOLEMN WORDS TO ISRAEL;

to the whole of this modern movement, with all its modern methods and developments and say:

> **"Behold, I will plead with thee, because thou sayest, I have not sinned. Why gaddest thou about so much to change thy way?"** (Jer. 2:35, 36).

The so-called "act of faith" only tends to glorify man; but it is a *life of hope* and not a "life of faith" which causes the Christian to forget himself altogether and to acknowledge that this is

A MORE EXCELLENT WAY,

and that God's way of holiness is better than man's.

The Road to Holiness 68

DR. A. SAPHIR ON HEBREWS 3:1

"Wherefore, holy brethren, partakers of the heavenly calling, consider the Apostle and High Priest of our profession, Christ Jesus."

"Think of Him; gaze steadfastly on the Lord Jesus. Consider, ponder. Let your mind be filled with Christ. Make not your sanctification the object of your contemplation, the theme of your meditation. What is it? Do you with to ornament yourselves and to come before God beautiful, or as a sinner? Do you wish to say from time to time, 'I have made great progress; I have advanced many steps in my heavenward journey; I have got into the higher Christian life.' as people call it? Do you wish to come before God beautiful? Or do you wish to humble yourself and ascribe glory unto the Lamb that was slain? Where do we see Christ? Are we beholding the image of Christ reflected in our own hearts, in our own dispositions, states and phases of faith? Then it will be reflected in troubled and muddy waters; and unstable and uncertain shall be the features which meet our eye there. Or shall we behold Jesus in the glory of His excellence, in the perfection of His holiness, in the beauty with which God has adorned him?

"Are we not to look off unto Him in heaven and to know that we are seated together in heavenly places and complete in Him? Shall we say, 'Oh, if I was only more holy, less selfish, more patient? If I could only see more of Jesus reflected in me!'

"Or shall we say, 'Oh if I could always behold the Man who died upon the cross! If I could always see Jesus, the Lamb of God that was slain! If I could always remember that I am bought with a price and that 'He was wounded for my transgressions and bruised for my iniquities!'

"I will ask you still further, why do you wish to be holy? Is it to depend more on Christ, or to be less dependent on Christ? To think more of the sacrifice which Jesus made upon the cross and to know and feel –

'Nothing in my hand I bring,
Simply to Thy cross I cling!'

Have you not detected it in yourself, that sometimes, when you have given way to temptation, fallen into sin you wished to avoid – when you have, in the performance of duty, stumbled over the same difficulty as before – that a feeling of distrust, disappointment and despondency comes over you – a feeling of wounded pride and vanity, of impatience and irritation – and you say, 'I am not making progress; it is really too bad; I am always falling into the same low state'? And then the lowest depth of self-abasement and humiliation is to go to God and to find no change in Him; the same Fatherly love, the same High-Priestly compassion and grace, the same Comforter, patient and gentle and you discover that in your best moments as well as in your worst you depend exclusively and entirely on the grace of God, which saves the chief of sinners. In fact, you have only stood by grace through the blood shed for vile sinners. How much we need to avoid the snare of cultivating vanity and self-seeking even in our sanctification!

The Road to Holiness 71

"How apt we are to make a saviour of self! I am anxious and troubled about the unscriptural view of the Christian life of which we hear. Look at it. What was it in the Church of Rome that for so many centuries made the Cross of Christ of none effect?

"They did not wish to ignore or reject Christ's salvation and to make Christ of none effect. Do not imagine that grievous errors and heresies began, as it were, in a bad and wicked purpose. How was it for centuries in the Church of Rome? Christ was put in the background and the Reformers had to dig very deep and put away a great amount of rubbish that had accumulated – the gold and silver and precious stones lay buried among wood and hay and stubble – till at last they found that Christ in whom alone we must rejoice.

"Look at the theology of such a book as, for instance, *Thomas á Kempis*, in which there is much that is excellent, but which suffers from the radical error of not distinguishing Christ for us and Christ in us. These good men began to be exclusively thinking of Christ in them. All their attention was centred in that aspect of truth. They said, 'It is true, Christ died for us; but now we must go higher and according as we realise Christ in us, we rest and have peace.' It was by this well-meant praising of Christ in us that they forgot Christ for us. They saw that a hypocritical and superficial trust in the merits of Christ was a dead thing, which brought forth no fruit, which gained no victory over sin and the world. They therefore were anxious to see life and power. But they did not perceive clearly that our only power, peace and life are in Christ, who died for us and in whom we have perfection.

"By looking to their love to Jesus, to their imitation of His perfect example, to their resemblances to His holy image, they never could have true perfect peace.

"As a Christian never loses comfort but by breaking the order and method of the gospel, looking on his own and looking off from Christ's perfect righteousness, so he that sets up his sanctification to look at, sets up the greatest idol, which will ultimately strengthen his fears and doubts, though at first it may soothe his feelings and please his imagination.

"The young Christian is especially apt to fall into error. After his first zeal and love, after the spring and dawn of his spiritual life, when he is full of praise and strength, when prayer is fervent, when joy and praise abound, when love to the Saviour is ardent, when work for Christ seems refreshment, there generally succeeds a period of languor and darkness, when he is led into the experience, painful but salutary, that even after his renewal the old man, the flesh, is enmity against the Spirit and that our all-sufficiency is of God. Now it is for him to enter more deeply into the valley of humiliation to see more clearly the need and the preciousness of the blood of Christ, to ascribe more cordially and with greater contrition all glory to the God of salvation."

"He is, however, tempted to choose the path of what appears progress, victory strength and beauty; whereas God's saints say:

'Christ must increase; I must decrease.'
'Christ is comely; I am black.'
'Christ is strength; I am weakness.'
'In Christ is all good; in me, that is, in my flesh, there is nothing good.'

"The saints of God find that, instead of progressing from one degree of perfection to another, they discover in themselves daily more of that sin which is exceeding sinful; they behold themselves vile and cling with all intensity of faith to Jesus, who saith unto them, 'My grace is sufficient for thee.' They are saved by grace; they know Christ only as their righteousness and perfection; and even at the end of their earthly journey, of their labours and sufferings, they grasp 'the faithful saying, worthy of all acceptation, that Christ Jesus came into the world to save sinners, of whom I am chief.'

- o 'Rest in the Lord, and in Him alone.'
- o 'Consider the Apostle and great High Priest, Christ Jesus.'
- o 'Place your confidence and have your joy only in the Lamb slain.'

- 'Call Jehovah, Jehovah-Tsidkenu.'
- 'Day by day you are a burden to Jesus, and His grace alone upholds you, while you stand only in His perfection.'
- 'You would not have it otherwise.'
- 'And while you are looking off unto Him, you will run with patience the race set before you.'
- 'You will fight the good, but real and painful, fight of faith; you will crucify daily the old man, who, to our last breath, is enmity against God; you will have no confidence in the flesh but rejoice in Christ Jesus; and your life will be hid with Him in God.'
- 'And at last Christ will present His children unblameable in body, soul and spirit.'
- 'Then shall we be like Him; and then shall we have no more conflict and no more sin.'
- 'Faithful is He who hath promised, who also will perform it. Amen.'"

THE ROYAL ROAD TO HOLINESS

Man is by his fallen nature selfish; and therefore, is necessarily prone to be occupied with himself. And even Christians, who possess a New nature, are not free from this ever-present temptation.

This is bad enough in itself and in its results; but, when it is substituted for occupation with Christ, then a double evil result follows: - the true way is forsaken, and peace is lost; the false way is taken, and misery is found.

The soul is deceived, because Christ is not altogether left out. He is brought in but mixed up with self; and is thus dishonoured instead of glorified. He is not put first. It is "Self and Co." and Self has got to do something, to "surrender" and "yield"; or else Christ is powerless to help. So that Christ is helpless until Almighty Self makes it possible for Christ to do anything.

Do we wonder that this new-fashioned theology fails to accomplish the object aimed at? Are we surprised to find that this "Gospel of Surrender," which comes to us New from the West, fails to produce the solid Christianity and holy living which the old Gospel (which came to us from the East) has produced all through the ages? Ought not its very newness to have put Christians on their guard, and made them look with suspicion upon it?

Do they not see, now, that it is a failure? It is no Royal Road to holiness of life.

Like all human remedies "the dose has to be repeated" again and again, and even then, brings no cure for the real evil, no relief from the conflict between the two Natures.[48]

We have met with many who have been brought low by the use of these new-fashioned medicines, which are so widely advertised in the present day.

---

[48] For more on this see E. W. Bullinger's *The Two Natures in the Child of God*, published by The Open Bible Trust – details at the end of this book

For, while the remedies are used in vain, the disease continues to grow apace.

There is only one remedy; only one way; only one Royal Road.

But this is a very old Road: "the old paths," God calls it. Oh, that we may succeed in leading some to seek for these "old paths," the path of peace and rest, the path of righteousness and true holiness.

In our last issue we pointed out this Royal Road; and showed that the secret lay in the utter rejection and obliteration of Self in all its ten thousand subtle forms, and the occupation of the heart wholly with God and His Christ.

This is no new remedy for the inherent evil tendencies of human nature. It is as old as the Word of God itself.

"They looked unto Him and were lightened." is the description of those who use the remedy which God Himself has provided and pointed out (Ps. 34:5). And in the same Book of Psalms He has given us two "Cases" of those who tried other remedies.

These "cases" are given to us in two Psalms of Asaph. He was the one who went wrong in this matter. He forsook the fountain of living water and hewed him out cisterns of his own devising; and the end of it is told for our warning. The new remedies nearly killed him. He tried two of them; and the second after he had proved the failure of the first! "So foolish was I (he said) and ignorant." It is the same today and will be to the end.

Let us turn aside and read the Divine account of these two "cases." The first is given us in:

PSALM 77

Here the soul looks within, as thousands are exhorted to do today. Asaph engages in a course of Introspection. See how thoroughly he did it:

1. I cried unto God with **my** voice,
   Even unto God with **my** voice;
   And He gave ear unto **me**.

2. In the day of **my** trouble **I** sought the Lord:
   My sore ran in the night, and ceased not:
   My soul refused to be comforted.
3. **I** remembered God, and was troubled:
   I complained, and **my** spirit was
   overwhelmed. Selah.
4. Thou holdest **mine** eyes waking:
   I am so troubled that **I** cannot speak . . . .
6. **I** call to remembrance **my** song in the night:
   I commune with **mine** own heart:
   And **my** spirit made diligent search

What could be the effect of this self-examination but misery?

And so it was. For he goes on to ask:

7. Will the Lord cast off forever?
   And will He be favourable no more?
8. Is His mercy clean gone forever?
   Doth His promise fail for evermore?
9. Hath GOD forgotten to be gracious?
   Hath He in anger shut up His tender mercies?
   Selah.

Here is a "Selah," calling our attention to the break, and pointing us to the *misery* resulting from beholding one's own self, and from self-occupation. Well does it say "Selah." We have seen the cause for this lamentable condition of things. Now, what is to be its prevention and its cure? The next verse tells us:

10. And I said, **This is my infirmity**.
    But I will remember the years of the right hand of **the most High**.
11. I will remember the work of **Jehovah**.
12. I will meditate also of all **thy work**,
    And talk of **thy doings**.
13. **Thy way**, O God, is in the SANCTUARY:
    Who is so great a GOD as **our God**?
14. **Thou** art the God that doeth wonders:
    Thou hast declared thy strength among the peoples
15. **Thou** hast with **thine arm** redeemed **thy People,** The sons of Jacob and Joseph. Selah.

Here is another "Selah" pointing us to the Royal Road to peace and happiness. Misery was the result of his Introspection: and it must ever be so.

For what is there within any of us to cause us the slightest satisfaction, except what God has done? "His workmanship" (Eph. 2:10). "His new creation work" (2 Cor. 5:17).

Here, then, is the description of the first "case." We see the nature of the complaint: the effect of the wrong remedy; the miserable result; and the true recovery.

The second "case" is furnished by the same Asaph in:

PSALM 73

Here, it is not introspection; not looking within, but *looking around*. Looking, not at self, but at others. Occupied not with that which produces misery, but with that which produces *distraction*.

The Psalm begins:

1. Truly God is good to **Israel**.
   Even to such as are of a **clean heart**.

Now see what the effect of this is. Asaph is looking away from himself, it is true. The inevitable result of looking at others, and especially at others who seem to be "more advanced," is to bring us back to ourselves and to reasonings about ourselves:

2. But as for **me**, my feet were almost gone;
   My steps had well nigh slipped.
3. For **I** was envious at the **foolish**.
   When **I** saw the prosperity of the **wicked**.
4. For there are no bands in **their** death:
   But **their** strength is firm.
5. **They** are not in trouble as other men;
   Neither are **they** plagued like other men . . . .
7. **Their** eyes stand out with fatness:
   They have more than heart could wish . . . .
12. Behold, **these** are the ungodly,
    Who prosper in the world;
    They increase in riches.

What is the natural result of this occupation? He looks around and sees the righteous suffering, and the ungodly prospering. He sees the (apparently) needed one taken, and the useless, helpless one left. Naturally he gets *distracted*! And he exhibits this result of his mistaken occupation:

13. Verily **I** have cleansed **my** heart in vain,
    And washed **my** hands in innocency.
14. For all the day long have **I** been plagued,
    And chastened every morning.
15. If **I** say, **I** will **speak** thus:
16. When I thought to know this, it was too painful for me;
17. Until I went into the SANCTUARY of GOD;
    Then understood I their end . . . .
21. Thus my heart was grieved,
    And I was pricked in my reins.
22. So foolish was I, and ignorant
    I was as a beast before thee.

Now we come out into the light. In the "Sanctuary," all is made clear (as was in the former case, in Ps. 77:13). The presence of God sets all right. Looking unto Him he is "lightened." Now he gives up all other occupation and beholds only God. Hence he is able to say:

23. Neverthless I am continually **with thee**:
    Thou hast holden me by my right hand.
24. **Thou** shalt guide me with **thy** counsel,
    And afterwards receive me to glory.
25. Whom have I in heaven but **Thee**?
    And there is none upon earth that I desire
    beside **Thee**.
26. My flesh and my heart faileth:
    But **God** is the strength of my heart, and my
    portion   forever . . .

Here is a blessed height to reach. We have seen
the steps by which it is approached. And, having
reached this Royal Road he travels on to the end;
and tells us of his blessed and happy experiences,
which he sums up in these words:

28. It is good for me to draw near to **God**:
    I have put my rust in the **Lord GOD** (Adonai
    Jehovah),
    That I may declare all **Thy works**."

Here, then, is the end of the whole matter. And it
is nothing in himself or others – only God Himself
and what He hath done. We need only add the one

great lesson, and set up this sign or guidepost, which points out the way to the Royal Road, and say:

> If you want to be miserable
> Look within.
> If you want to be distracted,
> Look around.
> If you want to be happy,
> Look UP!

Occupy *your heart* with God, and with the standing He has given you in Christ and we do not hesitate to say that your "walk" will take care of itself. In other words, God's remedy is a specific, which will accomplish a certain cure; while man's *nostrum* will and must assuredly fail.

THE TWO NATURES IN THE CHILD OF GOD
By E W Bullinger

The Bible sees the Christian as having an 'old nature', inherited through generation from Adam, and a 'new nature', bestowed through regeneration by God.

The names and characteristics of each are many and various, including "the natural man" and "the old man" over against "the divine nature" and "the new man".

The conflict between the two natures is discussed with details of our responsibilities regarding each, and the ultimate end of the old and new natures.

Finally, practical suggestions are made for dealing with the old nature.

This book is published by The Open Bible Trust.

It is available as an eBook from Apple and Amazon and as a KDP paperback from Amazon.

ABOUT THE AUTHOR

Ethelbert W. Bullinger D.D. (1837-1913) was a direct descendant of Heinrich Bullinger, the great Swiss reformer who carried on Zwingli's work after the latter had been killed in war.

E. W. Bullinger was brought up a Methodist but sang in the choir of Canterbury Cathedral in Kent. He trained for and became an Anglican (Episcopalian) minister before becoming Secretary of the Trinitarian Bible Society. He was a man of intense spirituality and made a number of outstanding contributions to biblical scholarship and broad-based evangelical Christianity.

Some of the works of E W Bullinger published by The Open Bible Trust include:

The Transfiguration
The Knowledge of God
God's Purpose in Israel
The Lord's Day (Revelation 1:10)
The Rich Man and Lazarus
The Importance of Accuracy
Christ's Prophetic Teaching
The Prayers of Ephesians
The Resurrection of the Body
The Spirits in Prison: 1 Peter 3:17-4:6
The Christians' Greatest Need
Introducing the Church Epistles
The Second Advent in Relation to the Jew
The Name of Jehovah in the Book of Esther
The Two Natures in the Child of God
The Names and Order of the Books of the Old
Testament

For details of the above,
and for a full list of his works
published by The Open Bible Trust, please visit

www.obt.org.uk

ALSO BY E W BULLINGER

The Foundations of Dispensational Truth

This is Bullinger's last book and is his definitive work on the subject of dispensationalism. It covers the ministries of ...

- the prophets,
- the Son of God,
- those that heard Christ, and

- the ministry of Paul, the Apostle to the Gentiles.

He comments on the Gospels and the Pauline epistles and has a lengthy section on the Acts of the Apostles, followed by one explaining why miraculous signs of the Acts period ceased.

A hard-back edition is available from www.obt.org.uk and from

The Open Bible Trust,
Fordland Mount, Upper Basildon,
Reading, RG8 8LU, UK.

A newly typeset book, well presented in an easy to read format, is available as a KDP paperback Amazon, which is also available as an eBook from Amazon and Kindle

ABOUT THIS BOOK

Towards the end of the 19th Century E W Bullinger grew more and more concerned about incorrect teaching on 'holiness', and how it was acquired. Such teaching arose in certain new movements and appeared in articles in the Christian press of his day.

These studies were first written in the closing years of the 19th Century. Thus what he refers to a 'The Modern Movement' relates to what had arisen in the United Kingdom at that time.

However, some of those errors of that 'Modern Movement' persist today and so much of what he wrote then is relevant and helpful to 21st Century Christians.

Made in United States
North Haven, CT
02 September 2024

56728520R00057